Reading Primer

R_3

Caleb Gattegno

Educational Solutions Worldwide Inc.

Second Edition
Author: Caleb Gattegno

ISBN 978-0-87825-056-1

Educational Solutions Worldwide Inc.
2nd Floor 99 University Place, New York, N.Y. 10003-4555
www.EducationalSolutions.com

Table of Contents

a	u o a ou oo oe	i y ey ay u ee e ia ie is	e ea a ai ay ie	o a ho oh ow	a e u o i ou io iou eou ia ai ie ei ea	u e o i ea ou	o a au ou	a ea ah e	o oo ew ou wo ieu	e ee ea ie ei i eo ey ay is	a ai ea e ei hei ae aye ey	oo ou u	o a ou	I i y igh eye eigh	a ai ay ey eigh ea aigh au	o oe ow owe oa ew oh oo	u ew ue ewe	ou hou ow / oi oy / / o

p pp pe	t tt te ed d 't	s ss se 's z zz ze si	s ss se 's c ce sw	s z ge	m mm me 'm	n nn ne kn gn dne	f ff fe ph gh lf	v f ve 've	d dd de ed ld 'd	th the	th	y	l ll le lle 'll / l le 'll	w wh	k ke ck c cc ch lk	r rr re wr 're / r re 're	b bb be bu	h wh	g gg gu gh gue	sh ch t s ss c	ch tch t	ng n	j g d dge ge dg dj	qu	x

Word Building Table 6

u	oh	ou	ou	ou	ou	ou	ou	ou
a		ie		au	ieu			
		ia						

si	gh	ld	bu	s
	ph			ss

Table 6.1

four pour wart trough cough

cause because your could should

would wood photograph elephant physics

double trouble enough

courteous courage courageous

patient patience soldier

soup group lieutenant shoulder

beside behind below before begun

begin began sure sugar

mission Russian busy built

builder building business minute

John Johnny Johnson

spinach village climate

– Four courageous soldiers had enough courage to shoulder their regiment.

– The couple got into trouble in the doubles match but not in the singles.

– Today, only farms and small villages have troughs.

– Young Johnny said that the elephant was too big for such a small photograph.

– Before we begin, let's put salt in the soup.

– Besides, busy men don't think about building a business without enough capital behind it.

– The Russian mission began work at once.

– Dentists tell patients that sugar causes bad teeth.

– Should we want what we don't have?

– Next month they will fly to Africa to see elephants and to take many photographs.

– The mouse was running inside the physics building.

– He took his cat with him to the roof to watch the match on his portable television set.

– The giant jet plane was just above John Johnson's farm.

– "Upon my soul," mutters the fisherman, "I'll get these lovely trout in my basket and take them home."

– Young Alfred drank four lemonades and got sick. An hour later at his house the doctor saw him and sent him to bed.

– The brigade has a general in command. One of his lieutenants likes the soldiers and looks after them very well.

– The gypsy was a fortuneteller. Josh wanted to ask her questions about his future. But Jack wanted to find out if people can truly tell fortunes, and if so, how.

– When they came into the room, they found the gypsy alone, gazing into a crystal ball. The boys became silent. Jack had a glimpse of the concentration needed to get into the future via a crystal ball. Josh felt he would be told what he wanted to hear.

– After a while the gypsy looked at them and asked them to sit down. Josh was to go first, but before the gypsy started, she said to Jack: "You don't believe that I can tell the future, but you will see."

– Jack was very startled that she could read his mind.

ie	ie	ie	oi
		ei	oy
		e	

ze	sw	wr
zz		

Table 6.2

write written wrong wrote wring

wrung wrist wriggle wreck wretch

wrap wrapper wrapping wrench wreath

friend friendly friendship

answer sword sworn swarmed

oil moist noise boil

coil boy oyster size

gaze daze buzz muzzle

bier pier peer beer deer

field priest relief grief

grieved belief believe believed

received conceived conceit

recipe married carried

– It is wrong to write the name of Mister Wright as "Right" or "Write."

– I believe he got married in Paris.

– She wrote several long, difficult words, but all were wrong.

– He put the towel through the wringer, which wrung out all the water.

– Friendship is the most valuable gift from life. Blessed is he who has good friends.

– The president was sworn in. He answered every question with: "I do."

– The wretched girl was so grieved by the loss that even the priest could not console her.

– Did you see that recipe for oysters?

– We received the coil for the boiler. From now on it will make less noise.

– With her moist hands she could not wrap the relief parcel which was being sent by friends of the shipwrecked.

ai	ew	eo	ew	ew
ay			oo	ue
			owe	ewe

lle	cc	gh	c

Table 6.3

few	dew	pew	news
due	cue	hue	ewe
sew	sewn	sewed	sewing
brooch	owe	owes	
people	occur	occasion	
drew	jewel	jewelry	
ghost	gherkin	ghastly	
gazelle	belle	carousel	
said	again	against	says
ancient	appreciate		

– In that story two Russian soldiers see ghosts in an ancient mansion.

– In the winter when the morning dew is frosty, very few people can sleep out in the open air.

– The ghastly wound made people feel sick.

– The Frenchman said in perfect English: "I got a live gazelle for my belle."

– Gherkins are small cucumbers which are marinated and sold in jars.

– The jewels on that lady drew the attention of two thieves.

– Since most countries forbid duels, very few take place now.

– She stopped the sewing machine to take the brooch from where it was pinned.

– Colors come in many hues and shades.

– The seamstress says that she has sewn my pants' seams.

– Against my mother's wishes, I rode and rode on the carousel.

– There is no other word in English in which the spelling "ay" requires the sound it has in the word "says."

is	ea	ea	ea	ea	ea	ea	ea
		iou		ah	is	ei	ay
		ei		e		ae	ey
						aye	au

kn	gue
gn	ckgu

Table 6.4

great break they

may day gauge

meat lead read heat weak

tear tier ear year hear

chassis debris

wear pear tear their aerial

prayer Earl pearl earth heard

learn hearse lead read dead

spread heaven weather

heart hearth ah sergeant

pageant ocean foreign

contagious capricious

knee knew new know sign align

creative creature Seattle theatre

genealogy plague league blackguard

– They all came to celebrate May Day.

– "Great," said the challenger. "We will break the record."

– There are two ways of reading the words "read" and "lead." Which are they? Do you know where they are on the opposite page?

– Does hearth have anything to do with heart?

– Write a few words that have the word "heart" in them. Do you know their meaning?

– To gauge the air pressure in our tires, we use a special instrument called a gauge.

– The debris from the blast spread over several miles.

– If the weather allows, Earl will take Pearl to the theatre.

– In Seattle, the weak sergeant could only say, "ah," when he heard the news from the pageant.

– Creatures are created.

– The ocean liner belonged to a foreign company.

– He became anxious when the girl he liked seemed to him to be capricious.

ai	ow	ai	ey	hei	eye	eigh
	ho		ay	ey	igh	aigh
				ae	ie	ai
					eigh	

dne

Table 6.5

knowledge honor honest

Monday Saturday Thursday Tuesday

Wednesday money honey

marriage carriage

eye high sight lie height

eight eighth eighty eighteen

freight weights sleigh straight

main rain nail pail

maintain mountain captain

heir heiress mare hare

aeronautic aerodome they're

key quay

– The days of the week are: Sunday, Monday, Tuesday, Wednesday, Thursday, Friday, and Saturday.

– It takes money to hire a carriage for a marriage procession.

– Eyes rarely lie.

– He was not eight yet, but his height had reached five feet.

– Out of sight, out of mind.

– The rain made the air smell fresh and crisp.

– When her nail broke, she felt some pain.

– Bears are said to love honey.

– She maintains that she is the heiress to his fortune.

– There are only two words in which "hei" requires the same sound as the "ai" in air. These two words are "heir" and "heiress."

As diseases spread, they are known as plagues. A plague is something nobody can stop, something that kills many people and which no one can be sure of escaping.

In the past, plagues were frequent and were dreaded very much. Sometimes the disease could be passed on just by contact with infected persons.

Only a little more than a hundred years ago it was discovered that germs cause diseases. Slowly a way of controlling plagues emerged, so that today they rarely occur.

Today vaccines have been developed to make people immune to contagious diseases. Because few people die from contagious diseases these days, we speak of epidemics rather than plagues.

Meteorologists keep records of the temperature, amounts of rain, humidity indices, and several other measurable components of the weather. From time to time, we hear on the radio or T.V. that records have been broken here and there. For example, we may hear news of the highest snow-drift ever, the longest dry period in a century, the largest amount of rainfall in any one day or season, or the largest number of tornadoes in any year.

These records make us feel that the weather is not very friendly, that it is capricious and unpredictable. We do not know why this is the case.

There are people who believe that one day we shall master the weather.

a au ai i	*u o a ou oo oe*	*i o a u e ia ie ea ae is*	*y ey ay ee ai ei hi hea ois*	*e ea a u ai ay ie eo ei ae*	*o a ho oh ow eau*	*a u i io iou eou ia ie au ea ah he*	*e o ou oi oa eo ai ei iu eau ough y*	*u e o i ea ou y*	*o a au aw awe ough oa augh oo ou hau ho ao oi owa*	*a ea ah aa au e*	*o oo ew ou ui u oe ue eu ough wo ieu*	*e ee ea y ie ei i eo ey ay oe ae is*	*a ai ea e ei hei ae aye ayo ey*	*oo ou u o* *u eu ue*	*o a au oa oo ou ho ao oi owa*	*I i y ie ye igh eye eigh is ais ei aye*	*a ai ay ey ei eigh ea aigh et ae au e ee*	*o oe ow owe oa ou ew oh ough eau oo au eo ot*	*u ew iew eau ue ieu ewe hu eu eue*	*ou hou ow ough* *oi oy aw* *oi* *o*

p pp pe ph bp	*t tt te ed d tte pt bp ct cht th phth 't* *z zz*	*s ss se 's z zz ze x si thes sth s'* *'s*	*s ss se 's c ce sc st sw ps sce sse sth z*	*s z ge t*	*m mm me mb lm gm mn 'm* *m*	*n nn ne kn gn pn mn gne in on dne nd ln* *n*	*f ff fe ph gh lf ft ffe pph*	*v f ve lve ph 've*	*d dd de ed ld 'd t tt*	*th the*	*th the h t phth*	*y i j u*	*l ll le lle 'll* *l le 'll*	*w wh u o* *wh*	*k kk ke ck c cc ch lk qu que che cqu cch co kh*	*r rr re wr rh rps rp rt rrh rre lo 're* *r re 're*	*b bb be bu pb*	*h wh j*	*g gg gu gh gue ckgu*	*sh ch t s ss c sch sc che chs*	*ch tch t c che*	*ng n ngue nd*	*j g d dge ge gg dg dj*	*qu cqu*	*x xe cc xc* *x* *x* *x*

Word Building Table 7

x	sc	sch	gg	xe
thes	sce	che		cc
s’		sc		xc
		chs		
‘s				x
				x

Table 7.1

exit examination exaggerate

anxious anxiously anxiousness obnoxious

anxiety xylophone Xerox clothes

schist cache moustache

conscious conscience conscientious fuchsia

schism science adolescent

scene scissors scent muscle

convalescence coalesce acquiesce

axe except excellent excel

accept accident eccentric

vascular suggest suggestion

James's Jones's boys' girls'

— Do we exaggerate the importance of tests?

— This adolescent tries hard to develop the muscles in his arms.

— If you want to be called eccentric, try to do everything to reach excellence.

— Before exams we are usually anxious.

— The scene was set, the scissors were ready to cut the ribbon, but the president did not show up.

— With finesse, she told him to exit.

— Will James's father acquiesce and let him go?

— There are many sciences, but we only study physics, chemistry, and biology at school. In these subjects we may also take exams.

— A guilty conscience creates anxiety.

— The girls' team wears fuchsia sweatshirts.

— Except for this article, I accept it all.

— That scent seemed obnoxious to me, but he loved it.

— Schist starts with "sch," like school and schedule, but sounds very different.

au ou ough ough ough ough ough

augh oe

aw

awe

n

Table 7.2

through slough slough shoe

though although dough

thorough thoroughly

thought ought sought nought naught

brought fought caught taught

daughter raw saw lawn

awful awfully dawn

law lawyer awe

laugh laughter laughing

hiccup hiccough

bough bow cough

wouldn't couldn't shouldn't

– Everybody was laughing, but his laughter was loudest.

– It was through laughing, while thoroughly mixing the dough his daughter had brought, that the old man fell into the slough.

– "Hiccup" is also spelled "hiccough," as if it referred to cough.

– My daughter taught me to skate.

– Nought is another name for zero.

– In the expression "comes to naught," the last word means nothing, and the whole phrase means that something was done without any result.

– Sought is the past tense of seek.

– I was in awe when I saw the rawness of the wound.

– "Bough," pronounced like "bow," as in "take a bow," is a name for a large branch of a tree.

– Although he is thorough, he gets through before anyone.

– I thought she felt awful and that I ought to take her home.

All through the night the fishermen fought the heavy seas. The waves were thirty feet high and swept over the entire boat, even above the funnels. Their boat was tossed about as if it were a cork. Only the struggle for survival kept those fishermen from feeling sick and made them find the energy to hold onto the wet ropes and not to slide on the wet floors or decks.

In the rain no one could see very much. The sirens were blowing all the time to let other boats know they were there. As dawn broke, the winds abated and the swell was less powerful. Hope came to the hearts of the men and renewed their energy.

Modern electronic technology has changed our world much more than the industrial revolution did about two hundred years ago. The first revolution was based on the uses of energy made possible first by the steam engine and later by electricity.

Of course, the electronic revolution was built on top of the first. So we still use waterfalls, turbines, and motors in modern plants.

The huge number of businesses that have computers and computer-directed operations are changing the way we think of work. Now, we leave the hard tasks to machines and mainly offer to humans the jobs of directing them.

It's not easy to see how different the world will be 25 years from now.

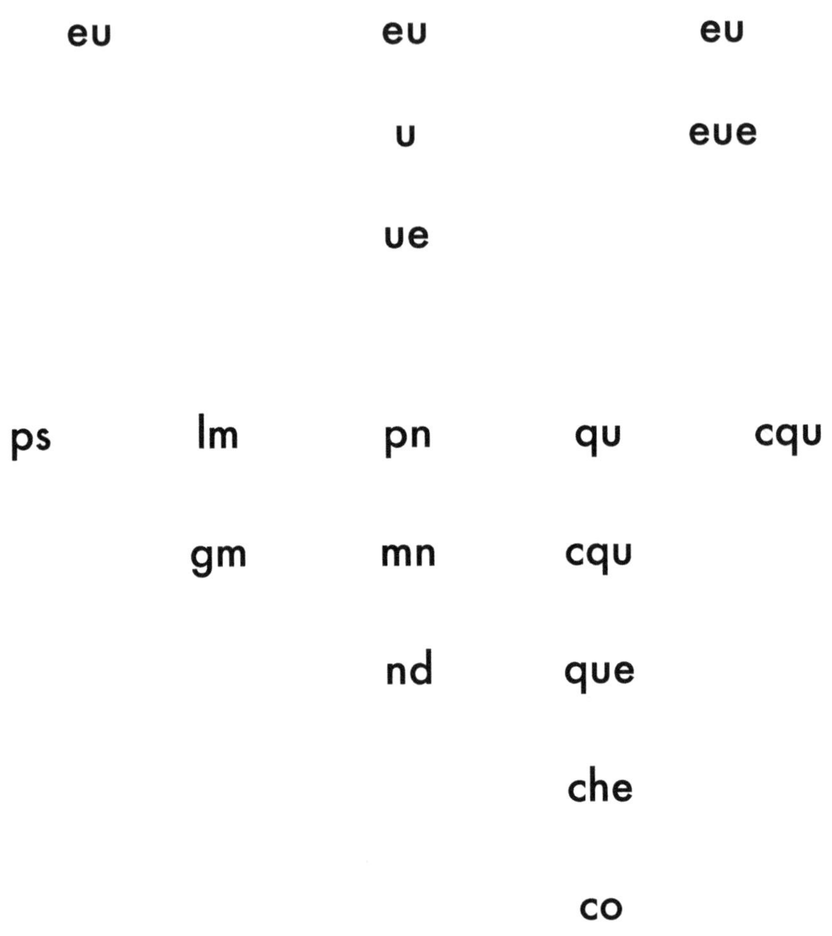

eu	eu	eu
	u	eue
	ue	

ps	lm	pn	qu	cqu
	gm	mn	cqu	
		nd	que	
			che	
			co	

Table 7.3

Euclid feud feudal

cube queue queuing

Europe cure puerile

lacquer clique pique plaque

ache chocolate

acquire acquaintance

pneumonia pneumatic mnemonic

grandfather grandmother

psalm palm alms salmon

almonds almoner almost

diaphragm diagram

phlegm phlegmatic

– In feudal Europe most of the wars were between barons.

– School geometry is mainly Euclidian, that is, as Euclid taught it in Alexandria over two thousand years ago.

– By being acquainted with him, I acquired a great deal that I can use every day.

– My grandparents are my two grandmothers and my two grandfathers.

– The words obnoxious, mnemonic, pneumatic, and phlegmatic are used on rare occasions, but I know them.

– Pneumonia was a fatal condition, but now it is much better controlled with drugs.

– Diaphragm is the name of the flat, wide muscle that separates the abdomen from the thorax. It is also the name of the window that closes the opening in front of a photographic lens.

– From "psyche," the Greek word for mind, a new science was created called psychology.

– Cues are used in playing pool. Queues are lines that people make.

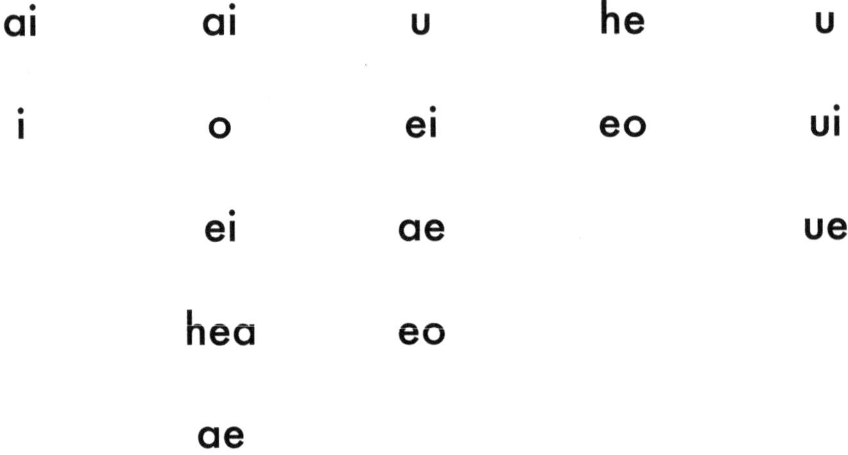

ai	ai	u	he	u
i	o	ei	eo	ui
	ei	ae		ue
	hea	eo		
	ae			

m	u	rh	nd
	o		ngue

Table 7.4

plaid meringue

suite choir language

village luggage garbage

women portrait forfeit

forehead sundae caesarean

bury burial

heifer aesthetic

leopard jeopardy jeopardize

vehement pigeon dungeon

tongue handkerchief

flu flute fluke Honolulu

fruit suit pursuit blue

rhythm rhubarb rheumatism

rhododendron

– There are thousands of languages spoken on our planet. Many of them are called dialects of some major language.

– "Forehead" has two pronunciations. Do you know what they are?

– Pigeons have been used as messengers, sometimes by prisoners held in dungeons.

– Sometimes languages are called tongues.

– These days many women work both outside and inside the home.

– I felt the rhythm of the wind in the rhododendrons.

– It was chilly when the choir sang in the open air. Some people had brought plaid blankets to cover their legs.

– Caesarean comes from Caesar, the roman emperor and great captain.

– Honolulu is the capital and main city of Hawaii.

– Fruit appears in a number of paintings which can be called portraits of fruit.

– Both men and women sometimes wear suits to work.

oa	owa	ei
eou	oa	

tte	st	t	mn	i	c	bu
th	c		mb	u	che	pb
cht					t	

Table 7.5

cigarette serviette

Thomas Thames thyme yacht

cello niche

hymn column lamb dumb

buy buyer buoy raspberry

toward cupboard cardboard

veil vein reign

either neither weird pierced

onion champion reunion vacuum

William listen fasten

vulture adventure righteous

pencil rhinoceros acid ceiling

equation

– The royal yacht went up the Thames to London.

– Paper napkins are also called serviettes.

– Twelve tame leopards were shown at the circus.

– Either goes with or; neither, with nor.

– The needle-like leaves of the yew pricked his vein and poisoned him.

– As a buyer for that big store, I travel a lot looking for good buys.

– The weird sound pierced the air and woke us up.

– For that adventure, she covered her face with a veil, a custom which had been abandoned since the reign of the last monarch.

– The champion showed a righteous indignation when his medal was given to someone else.

– Vultures, hyenas, and coyotes are scavengers.

– Rhinoceroses, hippopotamuses, and elephants are called pachyderms, meaning "thick-skinned."

– Although it brings tears to a cook's eyes, onion is used extensively in cooking.

– The committee hoped that the class reunion would not be a failure.

There are so many stories told by so many writers. Some are very moving, others very exciting. Some stories are about events, others tell what people think in the particular circumstances of their lives.

Since all of us are unique and special, we could each write lots of good stories. This would happen if we developed our sense of observation, particularly of what is fun or what is special. We can make a story out of anything, if we can say it without boring the listeners. If we use as few words as are necessary, and choose the right ones for what we want to say, then our writing will be appealing to others.

When we listen to a story, we are struck by different things at different times. For this reason, we go back to hear it or read it again. Good stories are those you want to read again and again.

However much we think that we should not believe in fairies, we all keep fairies as our companions in our mind. From time to time when we are alone, we call out to them, express our wishes, and hope that they will be heeded. That is, we hope our wishes will be heard and responded to as we wish.

Our own fairy is very familiar to us, even if we do not think of her as wearing a dress, having a halo around her head, or carrying a magic wand that can transform what she touches. Still, we whisper to ourselves so that no one else can hear: "let this happen," or "give me the opportunity to show how good I am," or "let my ticket be the one which wins a prize," or "let so-and-so be impressed by me," or "let me succeed in being as good as people want me to be." There is a name for all this: "wishful thinking."

But it's nice that the child we were is still alive in us today, however old we may be.

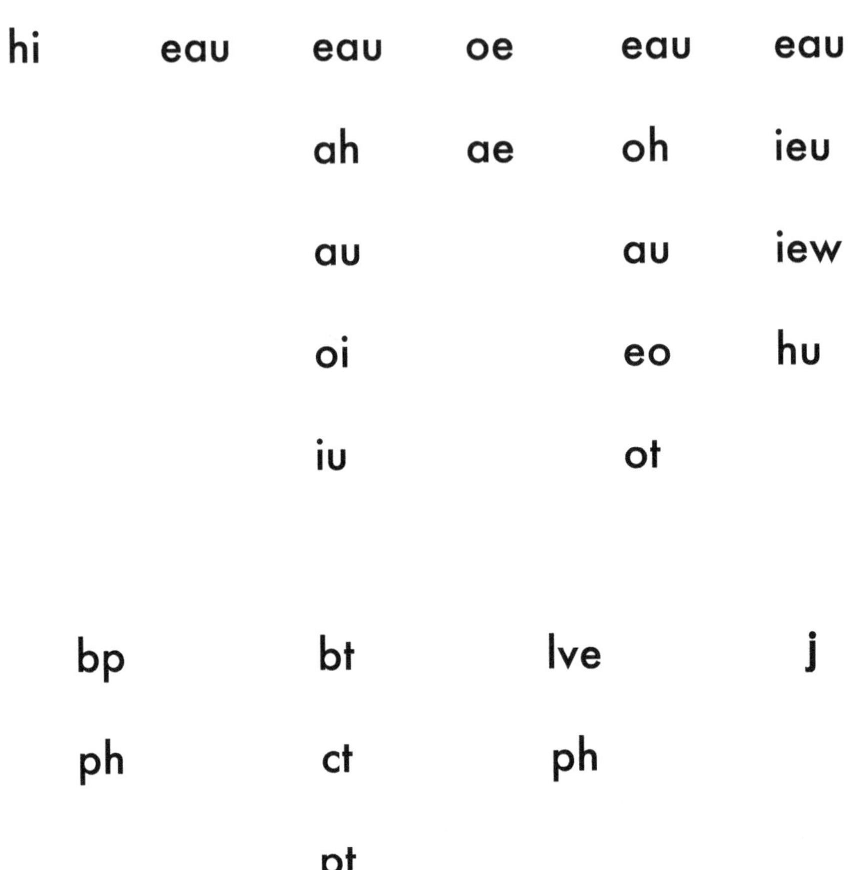

hi	eau	eau	oe	eau	eau
		ah	ae	oh	ieu
		au		au	iew
		oi		eo	hu
		iu		ot	

bp	bt	lve	j
ph	ct	ph	
	pt		

Table 7.6

beauty beautiful

adieu view exhume

plateau beau oh ohm

mauve yeoman depot

bureaucracy bureaucrat

hallelujah rajah

restaurant porpoise nasturtium

amoeba subpoena aegis

shepherd

debt doubt indict receipt

exhibition exhilarate vehicle

halves calves wolves

Stephen

– The numerous rajahs of India lost all their power as kings when India became a republic.

– Bureaucrats are all civil servants who work from a desk and handle official papers.

– The view from their front window was beautiful. They purchased the house mainly because of the beauty of the landscape.

– Amoebae are tiny animals of only one cell, which float around looking for their nourishment.

– Modern vehicles come in many shapes, sizes and colors.

– An ohm is a measure of electrical resistance named for the German scientist who studied this subject first.

– The indicted criminal was convicted since the jury found him guilty on all counts.

– No doubt you are in trouble as soon as you have many debts, and have no money left to pay them back.

– Her beau took her to the highest plateau in the country. She said: "What an exhilarating climb!"

– The yeoman had a lovely voice and sang a remarkable hallelujah at the service.

– The government subpoenaed all the tapes.

y	y	au
		oo
		ho
		ao

phth	ln	phth	cch	rre	j
	gne	the	kk	rrh	
	in	h	kh	rt	
	on	t		lo	
				rps	
				rp	

Table 7.7

bizarre hemorrhage myrrh

myrtle ethyl mortgage

colonel corps corpsmen

dinosaur board door floor

exhort extraordinary

Lincoln champagne

phthalein phthisic

absinthe eighth Southampton

Bacchus saccharine

trekked bookkeeping khaki

iron Jose

– A colonel is an officer in charge of a regiment.

– When they buy a house, most people borrow money. Then they say they have a mortgage on that house.

– The very rare words phthalein and phthisic are used in chemistry and medicine.

– He had a most extraordinary Lincoln, built especially for him for a very high price.

– When accounts are kept well, mistakes occur only on rare occasions.

– To sweeten their coffee, the corps of engineers mainly use saccharine.

– Absinthe is an extremely strong liqueur.

– In many armies khaki is used as a color for uniforms because it looks like sand.

– Bacchus is the Latin name of a Greek god.

– People engaged in the Peace Corps are called corpsmen.

– Myrtle is a plant which forms shrubs. Myrrh is extracted from other kinds of shrubs to make incense.

– We bathe in pools when we cannot go to lakes or seas.

– "Blithe" is another way of saying "blissful," but it does not refer to the loftier states of the person.

ois	hau	aa	is	oi	et
ea	oa		ais		e
			ei		ee
			ye		ae
			aye		

z	sth	sth	ft	x
zz		z	ffe	
			pph	

Table 7.8

island isle aisle

either neither dye rye aye

chamois guinea

exhaust exhaustion broad

luxury luxurious

ballet bouquet

suede fiancee Israeli

asthma isthmus isthmian

often soften

different difference giraffe sapphire

reservoir memoirs repertoire

waltz seltzer bazaar

schizophrenia pizza paparazzi

– The British Isles are a number of islands in the most northwestern corner of Europe.

– The English language used in the British Isles gave rise to many different dialects spoken all over the world.

– In British English, the words either and neither use the sound of "I" as the first vowel.

– The four words ballet, bouquet, depot, and chassis were borrowed from French. So were many other English words such as veal, mutton, and gigot.

– Asthma is a nervous condition characterized by great difficulty in breathing.

– Aisles between rows of seats serve as passages in planes, theaters, and other public places.

– To gain her favor, he bought her a sapphire. When he gave it to her she only replied, "Do it more often."

– At that school bazaar we attended they had a cupboard full of rye bread.

– An isthmus is a narrow passage of land between two seas, such as the Isthmus of Suez in Egypt.

– She died of exhaustion after waltzing uninterruptedly for fifteen hours.

– We can now read almost all the words of the English language.

– Many of them are not easy to spell because each sound can be written in so many forms and each form sounded in so many ways.

– We have met about four hundred forms for fifty-nine sound groupings needed for reading. Thirty-seven are pure sounds and twenty-two are combinations of two of these.

– Because we have met each sound associated with one color all along in our work with the charts, we can imagine the color for each special sound.

– In our Word Building Tables we have found how to put together the various forms that give one sound. We separated the vowels (which have sounds of their own) and the other signs that form syllables with the vowels. These last signs we call consonants because they need vowels to form sounds. All these tables are part of the Fidel phonic code.

– We found twenty-three sounds for the vowels and over two hundred different ways to spell them.

– We found about one hundred and ninety-nine signs for the consonants and organized them into thirty-six sound groups.

– The written form of the English language which we speak makes use of all the signs that we found in these books, the charts, and the World Building Tables.

– To write the English language as we should, we must practice reading aloud to see if we can give the right sound to the various shapes we look at.

– The better we can do that, the easier it will be for us when we want to write what we are thinking about.

– The second visual dictation game we played showed us how many more sentences we could form than seemed possible to begin with.

– In this way we learned to write new things until we could write anything we wished.

– When we can use the textbooks at school to increase our knowledge and gain new experiences, and use writing as a means of expressing ourselves, then we can say that we have a good knowledge of English. For this to happen faster, the exercises of the worksheets will be of great help.

– This is what we have tried to achieve in this work under the name of Words in Color.

Names for the Shapes of Letters or Alphabet

Read the part of each word that is underlined and you will find the name given to each of the 26 letters of the English alphabet.

a is called eight

b is called bee

c is called sea

d is called deal

e is called eve

f is called effort

g is called gee

h is called eightch

i is called I

j is called jay

k is called kay

l is called elephant

m is called empire

n is called end

o is called oh

p is called pea

q is called cube

r is called are

s is called esteem

t is called tea

u is called you

v is called veal

w is called double you

x is called extra

y is called why

z is called zero

CAPITALS

a A	j J	s S
b B	k K	t T
c C	l L	u U
d D	m M	v V
e E	n N	w W
f F	o O	x X
g G	p P	y Y
h H	q Q	z Z
i I	r R	

All the signs of the visual dictation pages can be put in the form of capitals by using the corresponding capital above as the first letter of the word. For example, for photo write Photo.

Every sentence in English starts with a capital. Names of people, countries, rivers, mountains, cities, towns, villages and companies also begin with a capital. In English, many adjectives start with capitals anywhere in sentences if they refer to the inhabitants of a country.

______, 20___

Dear Daddy,

Thank you for your letter and your lovely present. I am sorry you are still travelling. Come back soon.

My birthday party next Sunday is going to be great fun. I asked a number of my schoolmates, and their parents have accepted and will bring them.

Oh! Daddy, it is nice to think of what each will being to the party; what we shall give them in return; how to arrange the table around the birthday cake. Don't you think so?

I shall have for everyone: a notebook and a ball point pen; a colored balloon (each of a funny shape to make us laugh); little bars of chocolate. Do you think they will like that?

We shall play games, indoors if it is raining and in the garden if it is nice.

Daddy! Don't tell me that I am dreaming and that all that is too expensive; don't tell me to think rather of all the little children of the world who are in need of food and clothes. I know you are right and that it would be better to forget about my birthday party, but since it comes only once a year, let's be happy then and think of sad things the other days! Do you agree, Daddy?

Come back soon.

With much love from your daughter.

A Closing Statement

In the small space of these three booklets, we have condensed a study of English that is as complete as you may need for the expression of what you want to tell. Most spellings of English have been met in one or more examples, and their place in the Fidel provides the sounds that go with them. By looking at each word carefully and imagining with your eyes shut the shape of the sequence of letter in each, you will give yourself the best basis for becoming a good speller of English. If you know how to say a word and if the sounds trigger the shape conversely, you have made yourself into a good speller.

If you are prepared to take a pen and put down on paper what you ware able to say, you will put yourself on the road to becoming a writer. If you develop a sense of what sounds good and what can make people visualize what you say in words, you will be advancing on that road which all good writers take and which leads to their success.

www.ingramcontent.com/pod-product-compliance
Lightning Source LLC
Chambersburg PA
CBHW080937040426
42443CB00015B/3444
* 9 7 8 0 8 7 8 2 5 0 5 6 1 *